DESERT
ANIMALS
Searchin'
for Shade

Collared Lizard

by Karen Ang

Consultants:

Jim Rorabaugh, Herpetologist
Tuscon Herpetological Society
Tucson, Arizona

Craig Ivanyi, Executive Director
Arizona-Sonora Desert Museum
Tucson, Arizona

BEARPORT
PUBLISHING

New York, New York

Credits

Cover, © Joe Farah/Shutterstock; TOC, © Brent Landreth/Alamy; 4–5, © Joe Farah/Shutterstock; 7, © Danny Hancock/500pxPrime; 8, © Jo Ann Snover/Shutterstock; 9, © Robert Shantz/Alamy; 10, © Anton Foltin/Shutterstock; 11, © David A. Northcott/Corbis; 12T, © Melinda Fawver/Shutterstock; 12ML, © Eric Isselee/Shutterstock; 12MR, © Anat Chant/Shutterstock; 12B, © John Cancalosi; 13, © Joe McDonald/Corbis; 14, © azuswebworks/Shutterstock; 15, © John Cancalosi/Gettyimages; 16L, © Kenney, Brian P./Animals Animals/Earth Scenes; 16R, © Paul & Joyce Berquist; 17, © Leszczynski, Zigmund/Animals Animals/Earth Scenes; 18, © Leszczynski, Zigmund/Animals Animals/ Earth Scenes; 19, © Leszczynski, Zigmund/Animals Animals/Earth Scenes; 20, © Dave Morgan/Shutterstock; 21, © Daniel Heuclin/naturepl.com; 22, © Karen Ang; 23TL, © Brent Landreth/Alamy; 23TM, © Joe Farah/Shutterstock; 23TR, © iStockphoto/Thinkstock; 23BL, © azuswebworks/Shutterstock; 23BM, © John Cancalosi; 23BR, © Matt Jeppson/Shutterstock.

Publisher: Kenn Goin
Senior Editor: Joyce Tavolacci
Creative Director: Spencer Brinker
Design: Alix Wood
Photo Researcher: Michael Win

Library of Congress Cataloging-in-Publication Data

Ang, Karen.
  Collared lizard / by Karen Ang.
     pages cm. — (Desert animals : searchin' for shade)
  Includes bibliographical references and index.
  ISBN 978-1-62724-537-1 (library binding) — ISBN 1-62724-537-5 (library binding)
  1. Collared lizards—Juvenile literature. I. Title.
  QL666.L237A54 2015
  597.95—dc23
                              2014038699

For more information, write to Bearport Publishing Company, Inc., 45 West 21st Street, Suite 3B, New York, New York 10010. Printed in the United States of America.

10 9 8 7 6 5 4 3 2 1

Contents

 In the Sun

The morning sun is shining brightly in the desert.

A colorful collared lizard **basks** on a large rock near a cactus.

Later, the day gets hotter.

The lizard will go off to rest in the shade of some plants.

A Desert Home

Collared lizards live in desert areas as well as in other parts of the United States.

During the day, temperatures in the desert can soar higher than 120°F (49°C).

Spiky plants, such as cactuses and yuccas, grow in the dry, rocky soil.

The lizard makes its home among the plants and rocks.

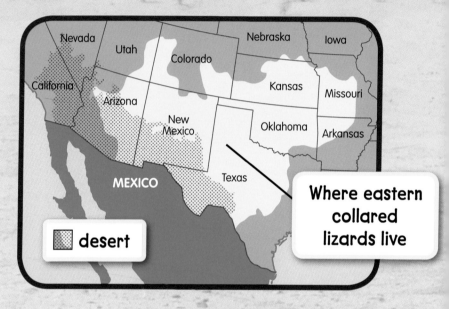

Where eastern collared lizards live

desert

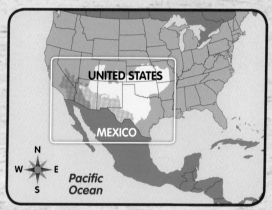

The collared lizard is one of many different kinds of lizards that live in desert areas in the United States. Like all lizards, it is a kind of **reptile**.

The Right Temperature

In the morning, the collared lizard warms its body in the sun.

The little creature needs the desert heat to live.

That's because the lizard, like all reptiles, is **cold-blooded**.

Its body temperature changes with the temperature of its surroundings.

The lizard will die if it gets too hot—or too cold.

morning in the desert

Without the sun's heat to warm its body, the collared lizard has trouble moving.

Where do you think the collared lizard goes at night?

9

Desert Nights

After the sun goes down, the desert becomes cooler.

The collared lizard must find a place to rest.

It crawls into a large crack in a rock or underneath a plant and sleeps.

The lizard rests until the sun rises.

What do you think a collared lizard eats?

sunset in the desert

The collared lizard has black lines around its neck, forming a collar. That's how the reptile got its name.

Racing After Food

A collared lizard hunts for food during the day.

It eats insects, centipedes, and spiders—and even other lizards.

To catch its **prey**, the lizard runs very fast.

As it chases its meal, it can rise up and run on its two back legs!

While running this way, the collared lizard uses its long tail for balance.

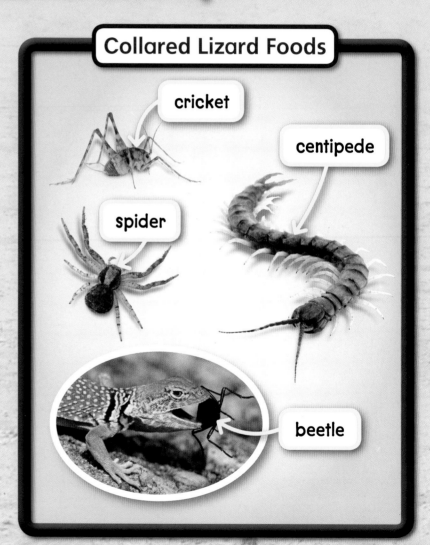

Collared Lizard Foods

cricket

centipede

spider

beetle

Desert Dangers

The collared lizard has many enemies in the desert.

Snakes, larger lizards, and birds such as roadrunners attack and eat it.

A collared lizard uses its speed to run away from **predators**.

If it can't run away, it will hide under a plant or rock.

The lizard may also try to scare a predator by charging at it with an open mouth.

roadrunner

A collared lizard can grow up to 14 inches (36 cm) long.

Starting a Family

In spring, male and female lizards come together to mate.

During summer, the female finds a safe spot in the dirt or under some rocks.

There, she lays up to 12 eggs.

male

female

Before a female collared lizard lays her eggs, her skin changes color. Red or orange markings appear on her neck and sides. The markings disappear after she lays her eggs.

female
collared lizard

What do you think
happens to the lizard eggs?

eggs

From Egg to Young Lizard

The lizard eggs hatch in late summer or early fall.

The mother does not stay to raise her tiny babies, though.

The young lizards care for themselves and find food on their own.

During their first months, they quickly grow larger and stronger.

By late fall, they start to slow down and eat less.

egg

What do you think happens to the lizards in winter?

Young collared lizards have dark patches on their skin. These disappear when they get older.

patches

The desert air becomes cooler in late fall.

By winter, it's too cold for the young lizards to survive aboveground.

They crawl between or under rocks and **hibernate** there.

During hibernation, the lizards do not move around or eat.

Then, when the desert warms up in spring, the lizards come out to bask in the sun!

Winter in the desert where the collared lizard lives lasts from about November to February. Temperatures can be as cold as 25°F (-3.9°C).

Science Lab

Create a Collared Lizard Habitat

Imagine you are a scientist who studies collared lizards. Create a model of the lizards' desert habitat.

How to make the habitat

1. Draw or paint small bugs or spiders on the bottom of the shoebox. Draw or paint a large sun on the inside wall of the box. This will be the collared lizard's desert home.

2. Use green pipe cleaners to make cactuses and other desert plants. Glue the rocks and plants down in different parts of the box.

3. Use modeling clay to make the colorful body and tail of the collared lizard. Bend the pipe cleaners to make the four legs.

4. Place your lizard in its home.

Use your model to show your friends and family how a collared lizard lives in the desert. You can even show them how the lizard can run on its back legs!

Science Words

basks (BASKS) sits or lies in the sun

cold-blooded (KOHLD-*bluhd*-id) having a body temperature that changes with the temperature of the surroundings

hibernate (HYE-bur-nayt) to spend the winter in an inactive state

predators (PRED-uh-turz) animals that hunt other animals for food

prey (PRAY) an animal that is hunted and eaten by another animal

reptile (REP-tile) a cold-blooded animal that usually has dry, scaly skin

Index

Read More

Houran, Lori Haskins. *Bloody Horned Lizards (Gross-Out Defenses).* New York: Bearport (2009).

Marsh, Laura. *Lizards (National Geographic Readers).* Washington, DC: National Geographic (2012).

Sill, Cathryn. *Deserts (About Habitats).* Atlanta, GA: Peachtree (2012).

Learn More Online

To learn more about collared lizards, visit **www.bearportpublishing.com/DesertAnimals**

About the Author

Karen Ang is an editor and author who has worked on many books about science, nature, and animals. She enjoys learning about different reptiles and, as a child, had pet lizards.